THE LEGEND OF THE
BROTHERSTONE

Also By The Author

THE SINGER TRILOGY
The Singer
The Song
The Finale

THE VALIANT PAPERS

THE PHILIPPIAN FRAGMENT

ONCE UPON A TREE

THE SINGREALE CHRONICLES
Guardians Of The Singreale
Star Riders Of Ren
War Of The Moonrhymes

WHEN THE AARDVARK PARKED ON THE ARK

IF THIS BE LOVE

THE
LEGEND OF THE
BROTHERSTONE

THE WISE MEN'S SEARCH

CALVIN MILLER

1817

Harper & Row, Publishers, San Francisco
Cambridge, Hagerstown, New York, Philadelphia
London, Mexico City, São Paulo, Singapore, Sydney

FIRST EDITION
Designed by Don Hatch
Illustrated by Alan Mazzetti

Library of Congress Cataloging-in-Publication Data

Miller, Calvin.
  The legend of the Brotherstone.

  1. Magi—Fiction. 2. Christmas stories. I. Title.
PS3563.I376L4 1985   813'.54   85-42784
ISBN 0-06-065711-1

86 86 87 88 89 HC 10 9 8 7 6 5 4 3 2 1

Contents

PROLOGUE

The Old Ones Gather

The young world shuddered in icy space.
The sun had died, the dark grew bold.
It is not the dark that kills the light—
The murderer of light is cold.

Balthazar doubted that the stars alone held the key to man's destiny.

"The city seems dead," said Kaspar. He spoke softly, yet it sounded like a shout in the ominous quiet of the night. White hair completely ringed the old man's broad face. His wide-set eyes were yellow with the years. He, like his two companions, seemed much older than the desert. The three of them were silent as the sands, speaking only when something needed to be said. But Kaspar felt it was time to break the quietness with conversation: "The city is as still and dark as the Arabah."

"What is worse," responded Balthazar, the oldest of the old ones, "is that the sky, too, is dark."

The glittering sky denied the statement. There was no moon, but moonlight could scarcely have added anything to the lavish incandescence of the heavens. The three looked up and then stared as one into the dying fire: disappointment coursed like burning caustic through the deep crevasses in their faces. In spite of a million glittering stars, the sky did appear to be empty and dark.

The old ones had built a roaring fire at midnight that now was little more than glowing coals on the desert floor. They had traveled for weeks together and had come to know each other well. The bonds that fettered them soul to soul came not as a result of lengthy conversations. Rather, each of them were star-lovers whose life romance was the study of blazing midnight skies. Thus, without speaking, their minds held spangled dialogue that made mere words seem void of light.

"I feel old tonight." Melchior threw the words into the blue-red coals.

"You are old," smiled Balthazar toward the dead and distant town. "But age is the father of wisdom—no man becomes a wise man overnight! Wisdom shatters faces with lines of age—eyes grow dim watching stars."

Melchior could not let the statement pass. "Dim or not, eyes are the windows of the universe. Devote your eyes to the night skies and, when your eyes are old, the stars will dance in daylight."

Melchior claimed to see the stars by day, and the others doubted his claim. Still they knew his eyes did see the flickering incidentals their own eyes often missed.

Kaspar changed the subject. "It seems years since we met in the desert highlands hundreds of miles east. The stars have never seen such lovers as we, and yet they fail us now. We are not only old, but a long way from our homelands."

The dark silhouette of camels rose behind their council fire. The silver trappings of their caravan glinted in the generous starlight.

"What's this, Kaspar, are you quarreling with the stars? They always win, you know." Melchior chided Kaspar for chiding the stars.

"I don't understand," said Balthazar. "According to our calculations, this should not have happened." His eyes narrowed to slits in his leathery face, canopied by his heavy forehead.

"What should have happened is that we should have made better calculations," offered Kaspar, stroking his beard.

"We are marooned by our own desire to find a new King!" mused Melchior.

"And the King of who and what?" interrupted Kaspar.

"How can the star just fade away?" Balthazar ignored the interruption.

The fading words stole conversation. An exploding ember cracked loudly, and the flare brought the three old faces into passing brightness.

After a long time, Melchior looked at the dark city rising at the edge of the horizon and then spoke again. "Why do you refuse to tell us why you have come, Balthazar?" His eyes left the fire and fell directly on the dark face of his venerable companion.

Balthazar knew he had delayed his answer overlong. The other astrologers had already declared themselves. They had come because Jupiter and Saturn were in brilliant conjunction within the constellation Pisces. This could only mean that the King of the world had been born in Palestine. But it was not these old familiar lights that drew them West. There was also a bright new special light too; a gleaming radiant independent star that baffled all of them.

Balthazar alone had come for reasons not bound to stars.

"My coming has nothing to do with Jupiter and Saturn; it is not even related to that special light," Balthazar began. "Three days ago, when we lost the special star we had followed all this aching way, nothing changed for me. Yet I could see doubt in the both of you." Melchior and Kaspar looked down at his rebuke.

"I did not doubt. For my confidence in this new King is not confirmed by astrology. Thus the missing star could not deny it. Too often I have seen men twist history into the stars. But the stars do not control our destiny. The stars, like us, are servants of a great mind—in which this poor, small desert sits, and we within it." His words came softly. Deep in his own thoughts, he slowly shook his old head and spoke again. "My friends, the star which led us has disappeared, but there is still great purpose in our journey."

"No man is wise who disbelieves the stars," interrupted Kaspar. He thought he recognized a sadness in the eyes of Balthazar.

"The stars are all. They are everything. Doubt the stars and nothing will survive. If the stars do not control our world and fortunes, all life is mad." Melchior, too, objected loudly.

Balthazar had to speak above their protests.

"See this!" he shouted, extending a dark stone. The night seemed somehow darker than it did before their hasty words. It appeared that he held only a desert rock. They could discern neither its shape nor meaning.

"A stone? What of it?" Melchior was still angry.

"It is more than a stone . . . it is a gem—an emerald, in fact," said Balthazar.

Melchior and Kaspar were suddenly silent, overwhelmed by the size of the gem in the palm of Balthazar's hand.

"Did you bring it as a gift for the child-King?" asked Melchior in wonder. Each of them had brought gifts as a symbol that they trusted the heavens.

"Like you I have a gift for the infant King, but this is not it," said Balthazar flatly. He closed the fingers of his hand around the large emerald. "Rather, I carry this stone only to remind myself that our poor world is loved. This emerald is a witness between me and an old enchanter who sings in the villages of my homeland. I bought this stone from him, for in many ways it seemed the stone and music were his very soul."

"He sings of emeralds?" one of them asked.

"He sings of *an* emerald, a larger one than this, you may be sure. Yet this one is large enough to call his song to mind that I may glory in his song's enchantment. As sure as I hold this stone, so sure am I this world is loved."

"For the witness of this stone you come to seek with us what the stars have already explained and defined? Are the stars not enough for you, Balthazar? Can you not trust the magnificent heavens, as do Kaspar and myself?" asked Melchior. "Must you, in your failure to believe in the stars, suddenly trust enchanters and singers?" Balthazar felt rebuke in the criticism.

"Hear me before you judge me," came the cry from the dark, wrinkled face.

"Tell us the enchanter's tale, then," demanded Kaspar.

"Indeed I will, and you shall see that this emerald is a small, faint image of the great green stone that blazed above a starfield so distant our poor eyes could never see it."

They said nothing further.

Balthazar appeared to slip into a trance. His face broke into a smile as his eyes closed to the world at hand. The years seemed to drop away. Lost in another day, when he was younger by more than half a century, Balthazar was a child again in a group of children, mesmerized by a teller of tales. With eyes closed, his lips parted. And where thick, slow speech should have been, a strong and youthful voice began a young man's tale. His story called the three old men to see a distant world; the Lord of all its spinning continents and seas was a King whose all-consuming pleasure was his Son.

I

The Green Fire

What deeds a boy will do
So that the skies above
May be the mirrored witness
That a son will risk for love.

"At last I'm on the mountain!" he exulted. "All my life
has been a rehearsal of this grand moment."

Prince Kyrris made his way beyond the city before the stubborn morning stars of Krissandor had fled. He looked beyond the pale horizon cut jagged by the mountain range.

"The day is born cold but clear," thought Kyrris, as the new dawn lit his way across the plains. "This day has spun a thousand dreams!" he cried aloud.

He gazed in wonder toward his goal. In the pale blue sky the Brotherstone was still green with bold fire. From his youth, the green fire had illuminated his world with a desire that beckoned him to climb. Year after year, it called him with a strong magnetism that would now test his young frame on the precipitous and sunwashed slopes that rose in vertical defiance to the snowy plains. Kyrris remained undaunted by images of the vanquished who had dreamed his dream and fallen. Like all of those who had tried and failed, Kyrris believed he could do it.

He spurred his fleet steed and reined its noble head to the east. He urged the swift animal on, feeling as though he rode the wind, which, mercifully was at his back.

By noon, Kyrris had covered most of the road across the plains. He patted his horse's flank as they rested and said, as though his mount could understand, "Those at the castle have not discovered our absence. The day is only half gone, and even if they have missed us they could not guess our whereabouts. Father may make the discovery by nightfall, but by then we will have a day's start on the search party that is certain to form tomorrow."

By afternoon, the Prince had reached the lower slopes. He turned his horse to scale the upward trail and drove him forward for another hour. At last he reached the Crevasse of Death.

Kyrris stared and thought, "You are a scar—a gash of hell across these lower cliffs! Warn everyone but me! My dreams are greater than my fears!"

Kyrris dismounted. Behind the saddle of his mount he found the warmer clothes which he had brought, and quickly put them on, drawing the hooded cloak about his face. He lifted the thin, strong filaments of cable that hung in golden rings, and tied the coil to his belt. He then pulled on his heavy gloves and looked straight upward, where the green light cascaded across the icy precipices that rose in vaulting walls of stone.

"At last I'm on the mountain!" he exulted. "All my life has been a rehearsal of this grand moment."

Ever since Kyrris could remember, his father, King Gerell, had looked longingly at the emerald light of Mt. Arras. He had seen his father grow more quiet throughout the years as he studied the aura of green fire. He knew that Gerell desired this prize, but could not guess the reason. Still, his father's need became his own! He must give his father the source of light: the Brotherstone! Now Kyrris was on the mountain at last. The dangers that it held did not occupy him. His very soul was

6

fixed on one desire, that his father would receive the Brotherstone!

He could not imagine what Krissandor would be like without the green light resting high on its pinnacle, dominating the night sky. It seemed almost to be a near star—yet what sort he could not fathom.

Kyrris did know that every attempt to bring it down had ended in disaster. Those who had tried to retrieve it had failed—not from lack of strength in their bodies, but because their forearms and hands, especially their fingers, failed them in the climb. When the fingers ceased to hold, the climber would fall and be lost.

Kyrris had long before decided to develop hands like talons and forearms as hard as the granite cliffs of Mt. Arras. His strength built year by year, as his body responded to the discipline of his dream. Of necessity, his first attempts at scaling the cliff were short. But by his twentieth year his endurance surpassed that of all his peers.

He concealed his exercise from his father, for he knew that the King's love for him was so great that it would never permit what Kyrris had in mind. Both men made their demands in love. The King, in his great love for Kyrris, had forbidden him to climb the mountain. Kyrris, in his love for his father, could think of little else, for he knew Gerell's desire to own the green fire.

His years of discipline were at an end. Now his test was at hand. Kyrris had set out secretly for the white cliffs. To scale them would require three days of his utmost endurance. He gazed with determination at the tortuous ascent to the summit where the Brotherstone rested.

Kyrris was well prepared. He wore more clothes than he would need during the day, because he knew the nights would be cold. He wore heavy gloves, for he knew the icy granite cliffs would freeze his fingers before the morning sun could warm his hands to life again.

He had tried over and over to visualize what it would really be like on Arras. Although the first snows had not yet fallen on the city below, the mountain was always ice covered. The aching hours would drag. Like a fly, he would hang on the ice walls while the full morning sun changed to afternoon shadows and then to purple-red dusk.

His arms would shudder, his tendons scream, in the agonizing hours of the climb. His strong neck then would barely support his head. He would need rest, but not dare to fall asleep. To sleep on Arras was to die! The chasms, like the jaws of a granite monster, would open to swallow him in his fatigue! The dark crevasse beneath him would become a pit so deep his fall would be a black descent into hell.

He made himself look upward. By night this same bright sky would hold the Constellation of the Crown, ten bright stars that formed the suggestion of a coronet. The starry pattern haunted him, for it settled nightly above the Brotherstone.

Kyrris abandoned his contemplation of the near sky as his eyes fell upon the Crevasse of Death. If he could endure, he would prove to the world that Mt. Arras could be conquered. He knew also his love for his father would empower him with strength beyond himself. Though he had never been closer to death, he had never been more happy.

"Oh, Arras, I love you for the treasure you hold. Your bright pinnacle is mine. Tonight I will climb—tomorrow I will stand on top of the world!" He exulted.

His joy was all anticipation; he thought of the King and cried aloud, "I love you, Father!" The canyons split his joy in diagonals of stone, and vaulting echoes startled the air with heady promises he meant to keep.

II

The Gift

Manhood never tarries long.
It overtakes a dawdling boy
And shoves him into age
And leaves him looking longingly at old and silent
    toys—

"I see the King's star."

"**H**ome!" said Prince Kyrris to his mount. He slapped his steed on the flank and watched him rear and snort as the great horse thundered away into the distance.

Kyrris was at last alone. He listened until the hoofbeats no longer resounded in the dark ravine. Then the Prince took a small grey bag from his tunic. He held it up, looked at it, and smiled. "Where other Gallactors have failed, I shall succeed," he boasted to the shadows. He smiled again and fixed the small grey bag to his belt.

Kyrris took the golden filament cable and unwound it to its fullest length. He formed a loop and tied a small stone firmly to it. He began to swing the rope in a widening arc, and the stone sang in the evening air. As he released the thin cable, the stone sailed in straight flight across the Crevasse of Death. The throw was accurate, and the cable wound strongly about a weathered and gnarled tree, securing the line across the void.

Kyrris took a deep breath and readied himself. Holding the cable firmly in his hand, Kyrris leaped without fear into the heart of the deep chasm. The rope held and Gerell's only son swung through the yawning void.

"When next I cross this deep abyss, the Brotherstone will be the prize of men!" he shouted to the cold, deaf blackness.

15

Kyrris knew he must continue climbing throughout the night. The Ledge of Legarro, his first goal, was halfway up the slope, and he knew that a few hours rest would be his if he could attain it. The ledge was a narrow shelf of stone, but it would provide a space wide enough for him.

The lower slopes of Arras were not as sheer as those beyond the Ledge of Legarro. Still, the word "slope" was not adequate to describe the steep outcropping of stone that Kyrris would have to traverse to reach the ledge. The gentler precipices beneath the Ledge of Legarro would not require the strength that he would have to spend on the cliffs that rose beyond.

The sky was beautiful, and in his zeal he rose swiftly and powerfully into the night. The stars gathered around the mountain. The light of the Crown fell against the icy stones and slipped and skidded down the mountain as Kyrris struggled upward.

On the more vertical ascents, his legs would tire. But when he stopped again to rest, he felt as though he could climb even to the stars themselves. His face and hands were aglow with the green, cold light. His noble young face was alive with confidence and strength.

Once he passed the rising walls of ice, his mind began to wander. How long had he dreamed of climbing Mt. Arras? Forever, it seemed. From the time he was a small boy he had looked at Arras with longing.

As he climbed, he sang an old song he learned as a child:

Life begins when the night hawks fly—
When the stars drop out of the pale blue sky.
And the evening star is born entire
In the raging flame of the emerald fire.

A child-like grin warmed his face as he sang, and
time raced backward. The world at hand faded; he was
a boy once more. Not just a boy, but a boy on the
most important night of the year. . . .

The Winter Festival had come. The crowd waited
restlessly for their first sight of the cold blue evening
star that would soon rise over Arras. The excitement
of the winter night had set the boy's round eyes dancing. Gerell had promised him a present when the day's
festivities were over.

"Oh, when will the star come . . . Hurry darkness!" How he rejoiced to see the sun swallowed by
the evening shadows.

The King's Festival began after the first snows had
fallen. The rising of the evening star over Mt. Arras
set the snowy citadel alive with joy. The crowd always
warmed the winter air with singing just as the first
star of evening climbed into the eastern sky.

Krissandor had known the emerald radiance of Mt.
Arras for centuries. None questioned the brave gleam;
none asked from where it had come; for every child
knew of the Brotherstone from infancy. At least, they
knew what could be known.

The Brotherstone was more than a "stone," it was
a gem—perhaps an emerald. The old ones in the

mountain village said that in the days before Gerell became king, an iron eagle with feather shafts of stone had laid the emerald on the peak of Arras. Gerell, like the monarchs before him, reigned in the green light.

Like a hundred other boys, Prince Kyrris searched anxiously for the star through the green light that crowned the distant mountains. His small eyes strained; he watched and fidgeted. He looked away to rest his vision from time to time. Tears of intensity spilled from his eyes as they sifted the sky for stars.

The King always gave the first child to see the star a special treat. Kyrris wanted to be the first to see the star! His eyes grew tired again, and while he looked away once more to rest them his hopes were dashed! A child's voice in the distant crowd cried loud enough for all to hear.

"I see the King's star!"

Kyrris wheeled and sure enough, the bright star rose slowly behind the green skies of Arras.

Kyrris was angry with himself. If only he had not looked away . . . But then, perhaps, he consoled himself, it would not look right if the King's son were to receive the Festival reward.

The boy who had cried out was Pellen, his best friend. Kyrris's own anguish that he had lost the prize was dispelled. He was glad that Pellen had won! And best of all, the Festival was born with Pellen's cry. As the star rose, the milling crowd broke into song:

Here is the Festival of Stars!
Now reigns our once and glorious King!
Come and behold Him
Whose splendor is light—
Whose scepter is joyous day—
Whose coming dispels the gathering night—
Whose chariots fly where the bright planets play!
Come children, come all!
Now gather! Now sing!
For this is the Day of the King!

The joy had come! There was merriment in the city of Krissandor. It would last for seven days. The fathers gave gifts to the children and taught them songs about the ancient light of kings. Kyrris's father, too, had promised him a present, and he was driven mad to know what the gift would be.

When Pellen came to the front of the crowd to gain the prize it was a hushed moment, for he received a brightly wrapped parcel. He took it from the King and tore at it eagerly until the wrapping lay carelessly in the new snow. It was a small iron eagle with feather shafts of stone.

"Oh Kyrrie, Kyrrie . . . it is an eagle! An eagle!" cried Pellen. He moved it through the air as though it really flew.

"Let me see it!" cried Kyrris. "Oh, it *is* an eagle!" The crowd behind them smiled at their excitement. The boys hugged each other.

"Oh, Pellie, you have won the King's prize!" said Kyrris in great delight. The boys played while the

King slipped back into the palace. Suddenly, Kyrris remembered his father's promise.

"You have your present, Pellie—but what of mine? Come, now, and let us see what Father and Mother have for me," cried Kyrris. "Let's go at once to the throne room. Come with me, Pellie, can you?"

"I must ask my father—I'm sure that he won't mind, but I must ask him," cried Pellen, running into the crowd to seek his parents.

"Don't be long about it," shouted Kyrris.

"I won't—oh, this is going to be a glorious festival," Pellen called over his shoulder as he dashed away.

The boys had long been friends. Their friendship never enjoyed itself more than when the Winter Festival would come. They loved to sled the lower slopes of Arras and listen to the palace storyteller tell of the coming of the Brotherstone in festivals long gone.

The old man croaked the rhyme that every child could say:

> It is the stone of kings,
> It is the stone of love,
> It is the stone of green,
> It is the stone that came to us
> Across the night of space . . .

The old bard would extend his bony hand and point a trembling, wrinkled finger into space and say . . .

Someday you'll see the green fire rise,
When the evening star is high.
Some wondrous night the skies will smile—
The Brotherstone will fly.

Kyrris believed the old man's tales and rhymes. He did not doubt that the stone would one day rise and soar.

The night was magic. Oh, where was Pellie! He had a gift and Kyrris wanted his too. His father was about to give to him something special that would mark the holiday with surprise. Why did Pellie not hurry . . . why . . . why . . . why . . . the star was high now!

"Where are you Pellen?" muttered Kyrris.

"Kyrrie! Kyrrie!"

"Pellie!"

"Father says I may go with you to see your gift."

The boys ran as fast as they could to the castle. Eagerly, they ran past the sentries who knew Pellen as well as Kyrris—for seldom had one of the boys gone anywhere without the other, and rarely did either of them walk.

They ran furiously through the throne room to the quarters of the royal family.

"Mother," cried Kyrris in excitement, "where is Father?"

"Where's your present—that is what you really mean, isn't it?" teased Kyrris's mother, Anzana.

Feeling rebuked, Kyrris grew quiet. Anzana drew

him near and hugged him, laughing at his sudden seriousness.

"Now, now, Kyrrie. I didn't mean to set your mind to doubting. Come—you too, Pellie—and I'll find you both a cup of hot berry wine." Her suggestion sounded as warm as the air of the night had been cold.

Pellen outran the Prince and his mother to the palace dining room. All of them were soon seated at a table large enough for a dozen of the King's Gallactors, drinking from steaming cups, when suddenly they heard footfalls in the outer chamber. Pellen watched Kyrris as he set his hot cup on the shiny surface of the long table.

"Father . . . Father!" cried the Prince, running to the door at the very moment that King Gerell entered the room. Kyrris held his father tightly around the thigh, for that was as high as he could reach.

He looked up to see his father carrying a large parcel.

"This is for you!" said the King, handing the box downward to Kyrris, who promptly reached up to receive it.

Kyrris saw that there were air holes near the lid. Was his present alive?

"Open the box carefully," warned Gerell, trying to look stern.

But Kyrris was too excited to be careful. He ripped into the box and threw the lid across the floor. The boy screamed as a red-orange ball of fur exploded into his face and shot past him into the interior of the room. "What . . . what *is* it?" Kyrris asked in wonderment.

Gerell and Anzana laughed. The frightened animal had shot out of the box and run up the wall, where it now clung in terror—defying nature—to the flat walls near the ceiling of the room.

Pellen smiled; he did not laugh for fear of hurting Kyrris. Kyrris looked bewildered as he stared at his festival gift, which now sat gazing down at him wide-eyed from its perch. He was as far from the boy as he could get and seemed intent on coming no closer. "Father! Please, what is it?"

"It's a Krissandorian ferret," laughed the King.

"I think you've frightened him," added Anzana.

Kyrris laughed too as, with a handful of sweet meats and soothing sounds, he finally coaxed the ferret into the tenuous beginnings of friendship. Kyrris and Pellen gently petted the ferret, and, within an hour, the Prince held his new pet. Stroking him gently, he told him what great friends they were destined to become.

After a while, Pellen left the castle and the royal family was alone. "What shall we call him, Father?" asked Kyrris.

"What do you think?" said the King.

The Prince thought for a moment. "I say . . . Khordez!" The King smiled at the choice. "Khordez" was an old word that meant "a gift of life." Queen Anzana smiled. . . .

Kyrris's reverie was rudely broken as his foot skidded on a patch of gravel. His right leg flailed wildly in the air before he regained his footing. The near accident brought the climber back to brutal, icy reality.

There was a patch of frost on the lower slopes. Kyrris shook his head. He was not at all tired, but the treacherous ice disturbed his mind until the images of his childhood faded and were gone.

III

The Darkness

They held the Prince to view in haste
The silent queen. He reached his hand
To touch the pallid marble face—
The weeping child was born a man!

"Father, the crown is heavy."

It was an hour beyond the middle of the night when Kyrris reached the Ledge of Legarro. He pulled the small grey bag from his waist, loosened his belt, and lay down. He was so tired the cold could not prevent his falling asleep; but his sleep was troubled.

In the mists of his fading consciousness he heard a voice singing a song he had not heard for many years. It was Gerell's voice singing a last lament:

> When the snow piled high on the battlements
> And the frosted turrets all about,
> Two sets of footprints entered the woods
> But only one came out.

His father's song lured him deep into a willful slumber . . .

The dreaming Kyrris saw himself, still a boy, as he stood beside Gerell and stared at a black hole cut like a jagged wound in the winter snow. The coffin was lowered into the ground. The Queen was dead!

The dark plague that none understood had taken her life. Hundreds had died, but it was Anzana's still, white face that taught Kyrris the anguish of death.

"Oh, Mother . . . Mother!" Kyrris sobbed, looking away in anguish. His mother's warm face seemed to float above the pallid visage of the cold, dead Queen.

Gerell caressed his son in a vain attempt to love away the hurt.

The King's heart was breaking too, yet he wept to see his son so torn. Kyrris was stunned. He never knew that kings cried.

"Yes, my son, kings cry," said Gerell. "And the greatest kings cry often." He held the Prince and saw his own face mirrored in the brimming eyes.

At last father and son turned away and walked homeward across the snowy fields. The King's boots crunched loudly as they marked the snow with the weight of sorrow. The King heard his small son's quiet sobbing. As the boy's tears touched the cold snow it seemed to Gerell that his son's grief was too great a burden for even a king to carry.

"My son," he said finally, "When princes grieve, kings weep."

"I do not understand father," said Kyrris.

"You cry because your mother has gone away. My tears come from the double grief of my own loss and seeing you so hurt." Gerell's voice choked to silence. At last he hugged Kyrris and said, "It's growing dark, we must get home . . . Look, there's the Brotherstone." The green light washed the sky and night came on.

"My son, the Brotherstone is the light of kings; someday you will wear this crown." Gerell stopped. He took the crown off his own head and set it on Kyrris's small dark head.

"Father, the crown is heavy."

"So is love," the King replied. The boy thought of his mother and the black hole in the white snow.

When they were alone in the castle, the fireplace became a spell of red flame. They watched in utter silence; the stalwart Gerell looked into the flickering light. His head sagged and his shoulders bent, even as he sat.

Prince Kyrris remained silent. Only gradually did both of them become aware of a soft thumping sound against the window. Kyrris turned first to look.

"Father, there's a dove fluttering against the pane!"

Gerell turned slowly. "The bird is tortured by the cold," reasoned the King, "and frightened by the night."

Gerell opened the window and the dove fluttered in, sailing across the room. She drew in her wings and settled on the mantle, just above the fire.

"Father, look! She holds in her beak the chain and emerald you once gave to Mother!"

"But it was sealed in . . ." Gerell stopped. "What mystery is this? The very chain I once gave to my Queen! This is surely a sign . . ." said the King.

Gerell took the chain from the dove and opened the clasp. In his agitation, he dropped the emerald. It fell almost to the floor, but suddenly, unbelievably, the emerald stopped in the air just above their feet! Slowly it began to rise, glowing like the Brotherstone. As it went ever upward, high above their heads, a brilliant arc of emerald fire cut a ribbon of light across their vision. Finally, it settled back again, dropping gently into the King's hand.

Gerell and Kyrris shivered, remembering the words:

> Someday you'll see the green fire rise,
> When the evening star is high.
> Some wondrous night the skies will smile—
> The Brotherstone will fly.

Then the light slowly extinguished.

The King was silent for what seemed an eternity. "This was your mother's," he told his son. "Now she has sent it to you."

The King fastened the chain around Kyrris's neck and snapped the gold clasp shut. It seemed overlong against the child's thin neck and chest.

"It will fit better in the years ahead," said Gerell. "When you've become a man."

"Oh, Father . . . I don't want to be a man! I want to see my mother once again."

"Nothing is lost forever. Wear this chain and stone against the day . . ." the King stopped. He took the iron poker and raked it through the glowing coals of the fire.

"Let's go to sleep."

The King walked Kyrris to his room and helped him into bed.

"May the fire of the Brotherstone comfort you, Kyrris."

The boy hugged his father as if he would never let him go.

Gerell snuffed the candle fire between his thumb and fingers and the room went black, then Gerell left his son. Kyrris listened until he heard the King's boots fall empty on the palace floor and knew that his father also was in bed.

Young Kyrris had never seen a night so devoid of light that he could feel the dark, but this was such a one. It was so black! Why would the blackness not go away? It seemed to move in on Kyrris as he drew the covers up around his chin. He thought again of the black hole in the white snow, and saw again the specter of his mother's silent form.

"It is dark . . . so dark . . . black and thick dark. I am chilled . . . what if my father should not live . . . then there would be another black hole in the snow . . .

"Father," Kyrris cried in fear. "Father, it is so dark . . . tell me that you yet live in the darkness!"

"I am alive," the King called back to the child prince.

"Father, I am afraid . . . can I sleep with you?" cried Kyrris.

"Yes, come . . . come, my son!"

Kyrris edged his way across the stone floor. The cold seeped into his feet. He could see nothing. Feeling his way along the corridor he came at last to his father's room. Moving across the floor he bumped the edge of his father's bed. The King's grief gave way to compassion, and he thrust his hands into the blackness, groping for his son's small frame. He drew him

33

close and held him fast. The child clung tightly to his father. After a while, Kyrris began to feel better. But when he opened his eyes, the blackness was impenetrable. It seemed that he could see no better with his eyes open than he could see with them closed. The dark would not recede. Again his doubts flew.

"Father . . . Father . . . It is so dark! Tell me if you live in the darkness." Kyrris cried.

"I am alive . . . I live in the darkness . . ." said the King.

"Father, do you look this way?"

"I look your way, my son." Kyrris breathed slowly in the swirling darkness, holding tight to his father. Finally, the Prince and King faced each other and slept . . .

Kyrris awoke feeling cold and much older on the Ledge of Legarro. The dream was a long time ago. Now it was nearly morning on Mt. Arras, and he arose and brushed the snow from his clothes. Lifting his eyes to the peak, he prepared himself to climb once more.

IV

The Watchers

My son endures the dark alone
Where the high winds wail and boulders groan.
O come, you comets! Pass the night!
Because my waiting son needs light.

The Watcher

"*Your Majesty, I believe someone nears the peak of Arras—there is a form against the light.*"

As he resumed his climb, Kyrris realized that the others must surely have missed him by now. He was certain that his father would have sent a party of climbers to search for him.

Kyrris was right. When his horse had returned riderless, the King knew something was very wrong. At daybreak King Gerell and Pellen and a company of men began to move toward the mountain. The King somehow knew his son's long infatuation with Arras now lured the Prince toward its summit. All day, as the royal search party moved eastward to the mountain, Kyrris climbed. By late afternoon, the sun of Krissandor threw broad and golden light against the mountain, which waited as always for the sun to sink into the western seas.

By nightfall, the royal company was camped beside the Crevasse of Death. Against the setting sun, Pellen studied the green light above him.

Something seemed to disturb the light. Pellen watched for a moment, and suddenly cried out, "Your Majesty, I believe someone nears the peak of Arras—I see a form against the light."

The King was on his feet in an instant. Gerell arched his back and stared upward. Suddenly, his lips parted and his face was torn by anguish. He breathed one word, "Kyrris!"

The King beheld Kyrris just as he came to the last outcropping of vertical stone. He was now less than a thousand feet from the Brotherstone, hanging like an insect from the icy cliff. The King could tell he still wore his gloves, and for this alone gave thanks.

"My son . . . hold fast, for I love you. . . ." These were the only words Gerell spoke. The men standing near him were silent with fear as they beheld all their King beheld.

The form that hung against the stone moved neither up nor down. Why had he stopped? Was he about to fall? The King could barely stand to watch, and yet he dared not cease.

If his only son should slip, his watching eyes would crack like porcelain, shattered by his own great love.

"Why does Kyrris not move up or down?" thought Gerell. The King stood mute and puzzled. Suddenly, he noticed a dark line against the ice-slick stone. What was it? Though he could barely stand to let Kyrris out of his sight, yet his eye moved up the slope following the line. From his great distance, it looked like a fine tracing drawn in ink, flat against the vertical cliff.

It moved up . . . up . . . until it rose to the very underlip of the pinnacle.

The King could hardly believe what he saw: near the top of the icy stone was a dark blur that looked as though it were an animal of some sort. Suddenly he cried out loud—"It is an animal—it's the ferret!" Gerell's face broke into a smile.

"Khordez . . . Khordez . . . It's Khordez!"

The other Gallactors looked as though the Monarch had lost his senses.

"Khordez, Khordez!"

He lowered his stinging eyes a moment.

"What a remarkable idea!"

"What idea?" cried Pellen.

Gerell did not answer immediately. Looking high up the slopes to make sure, his searching eyes saw all that he was about to report. He could see that the Krissandorian ferret, obedient to its master, had secured a loop around the narrow shaft of stone at the very peak of Arras. Now the King watched as Khordez moved rapidly back down the taut line. His vision raced ahead of the ferret and swept across the stone. Down, down, down ran the fine cable until it reached the Prince. Kyrris held the line.

Again the King's gaze was interrupted. His eyes twinkled in merriment.

"The line is around Kyrris!"

He laughed out loud now. "My son is a genius. He is tied to the mountain! He cannot fall . . . HE CANNOT FALL!"

Gerell laughed so wholeheartedly that he inspired a swell of laughter from all of those who watched with him.

They all watched the all–but–invisible Prince moving up the thin line. But it was Pellen who watched longest of all. Was it possible that Kyrris would do what so many others had tried and failed to do?

"He's moving up now!" cried Pellen. Kyrris was leaning outward from the cliff with his feet against the stone, his strong arms pulling him upward into the green light. The black shadows enclosed a bright joy. The body of a man was eclipsing the light of the Brotherstone.

V

The Pinnacle

While older men hold council
And long deliberate,
A fever rages in the young—
Impatience cannot wait.

"I love you, Father—the Brotherstone is yours."

Kyrris was exhilarated, transfixed at the heights! His only thought was to please his father—and the joy of such a thought released in him a power that brought him to the summit.

Khordez, still shivering from his lonely climb up the steep and icy wall of stone, now warmed himself inside Kyrris's tunic. It had been a long journey inside that grey bag, and he was weary—for though the rope was as light as it was strong, it had more than taxed the ferret. Now, however, Khordez could rest while his master put his body to the trial of rising up the rope.

At last the climbing went faster. The closer Kyrris drew to the pinnacle, the more he felt the blinding splendor. He wondered as he neared the peak if the brilliant light would burn his eyes.

But best of all, its light was warm. The last two hundred khronns of his ascent were free of ice. Kyrris decided that when he crossed this section again he would bring the rope two hundred khronns down the slope and anchor it.

His cable was a thousand khronns long, and the extra two hundred khronns of dry stone would allow him to move twelve hundred khronns down the vertical ice wall before he drove a second suspension stake into the ice. There he would wait for Khordez to untie the cable, and let it fall down the slope where it would be secured to the second pinion. He would have to repeat the same maneuver to bring himself at last to the Ledge of Legarro. From there on, the slopes would be easier to manage.

Lost in thoughts of his descent, Kyrris suddenly realized he had finished his climb. He was at the heights, and the fiery green Brotherstone rested atop the peak. He had only to reach out to touch it. There was a strong brilliance to the stone—it was dazzling but not blinding!

How odd it lay so simply at his feet as any ordinary rock might have done. Kyrris towered above it realizing that all his life it had towered above him.

Lost in the wonder of his accomplishment, he exulted and cried aloud, "I love you, Father—the Brotherstone is yours!" He grew silent with awe. How odd it seemed to stand on top of Arras. All his life he had looked upward into the night sky to behold the Brotherstone. Now he stood where he long had gazed, in a thousand dancing shafts of green light.

The air was warm. The green fire blazed, beckoning him. Feeling its fiery heat, he cautiously removed his glove and carefully extended his naked hand. He laid his fingers on the stone; the stone was not cool, but neither did it burn. Earth and sky were one!

Exultantly, Kyrris held the stone and raised high his aching arms. He extended his open hands and felt as though he touched the clear white stars. He lifted his handsome face to the universe and cried once more aloud,

"Father, I give this night to you!"

He lifted the stone higher than it had ever been, gazing at it in awe. Its emerald fire nearly blinded him. How long Kyrris stood there, he did not know. Finally, it was time to come down.

Kyrris took a leather harness from a pouch outside his belt. He fixed the straps around the Brotherstone and strapped it to his back. Even through his heavy coat it felt warm.

In a moment of insight, the Prince knew his coat would only make his descent more difficult. The light of the Brotherstone would give him all the warmth he needed. He removed the harness and the stone, took off his heavy coat and leggings, and flung them outward into space. They fluttered quickly out of sight into the darkness far away.

Khordez ran back up his leg into his tunic and peered out into the night. Kyrris smiled, remembering what his father once told him: "Khordez is a hardy ferret—raised on the slopes of Mt. Arras." Now it was just as though the ferret knew his plan—both of them were ready to descend, but they both needed to rest.

Kyrris decided he might as well rest on top of the mountain. He lay down on a flat rock that was just wide enough, and, for a pillow, Kyrris had the warm Brotherstone. He closed his eyes. Sleep was impossible, but he forced himself to remain motionless for he knew his arms and legs would soon know the greatest test of all.

He could see very little of the stars because of the bright incandescence of the stone; but he knew they were there.

What he could see caused him to remember the castle gallery. . . .

He would never forget the first time he had ever seen the great gallery. Gerell had been with him. The two of them talked alone in the largest room of the castle, the Hall of Heroes.

The first snow had begun to fall outside. All around the torchlit walls of the high vaulted room hung large paintings of faithful ancient Gallactors who once served other kings. Most of them had died centuries before in an attempt to reach the Brotherstone that lay upon the pinnacle of Arras.

As Gerell talked, Prince Kyrris sat beneath a painting of the Gallactor, Rengold, a hero he had long admired. He was the only man who had climbed Mt. Arras nearly to its summit. Some said he actually touched the Brotherstone before he slipped and fell.

"Why did he fall?" the Prince asked, looking upward at the towering image. "He was so near, and yet . . ."

The King did not reply. Instead he looked at his son with serious eyes and said, "You have a deadly fever, Kyrris."

"I feel fine, Father, really I do!" the Prince protested.

"You feel fine, but you have a fever. . . ." Gerell said nothing for a moment . . . then he continued on.

"The fever that you have has killed nearly all of these great men." He gestured in a sweeping fashion to the pictures and statues of the fallen. He went on talking. "It

50

pains me to understand your deepest wish. My son, you have the sickness that slaughtered all of these with great desire. You mean to have the Brotherstone, do you not?''

The Prince confessed. ''Father, I do! I want it not for me, but for you.

''Father, I have practiced long. I have trained for a thousand, thousand days. My arms are iron—my thighs can lift me up where eagles fly. I love you—I would gladly die to give you this great prize.''

''Kyrris, I don't want you to die for me. I want you to live for me! I don't want you to climb Mt. Arras. Promise me you will not climb.''

''Father, I must!''

''My son, I do not want you to risk yourself on Arras. Come with me now. I will show you my heart's great desire.'' The King then turned upon his heel and, followed by his son, walked into the castle gallery. The castle gallery was a large and dark room located beneath the throne room. It held a dazzling mock universe complete with even small stars. In the room there hung a sea of glittering stars and whirling lights where children stared in awe and dared not speak before sights so infinite.

''Here, my son.'' The King reached up and touched a silver world. ''This is Krissandor. Look. All the way across this spangled universe, there spins a rebel world.''

Gerell turned and walked away across the gallery. Stopping at the edge of light, he motioned to Kyrris, pointing upward to a tiny sun. ''Three planets out from that small star, there flies a tiny world. Upon that world are tiny little beings who regard themselves as great. They live in hate . . ."

"Hate?" said Kyrris interrupting him.

"Hate is a word I pray our realm will never understand."

"The world is so little. Can it be so all-important?" asked the Prince. But when he turned to face his father, he knew the tiny world was deeply loved. Gerell turned his face away. The distant doorway stood ajar, and comets sliced the blackness.

Prince Kyrris looked at the vast star fields above their heads.

"How many worlds are there which live in hate?"

"Ah, Kyrris, see all these swirling stars! In all this awesome night, there is but one lost world. Can you, my son, believe I love it so? There is no distance I would not go to save this fleck of light."

"But Father, how can it be saved?"

The King groaned. Once more he turned away.

"The green fire on Mt. Arras, son, has burned for centuries alone."

Kyrris remembered the child rhyme from long ago, and began slowly to recite it:

Someday you'll see the green fire rise,
When the evening star is high.
Some wondrous night the skies will smile—
The Brotherstone will fly.

"Your love for the Brotherstone is as deadly as my love for this poor planet. We both have a fever, son. I fear it is a fever unto death."

The King shuddered. A comet passed above them, streaked the sky, and died . . .

Kyrris's long-ago world faded, and he smiled as he opened his eyes in the green light. He woke upon the top of Arras. "It was not a fever unto death now was it, Father! I have climbed the mountain," he cried aloud.

He still had to make the perilous descent, but he held what no one had ever owned and triumphed where no one had ever stood. He smiled, walked to the edge of the world, and started down.

VI

The Treasure of Arras

No dream was ever void of hope—
No mountain scaled by coils of rope.
A prince must prove his fledgling hand
For every king was first a man.

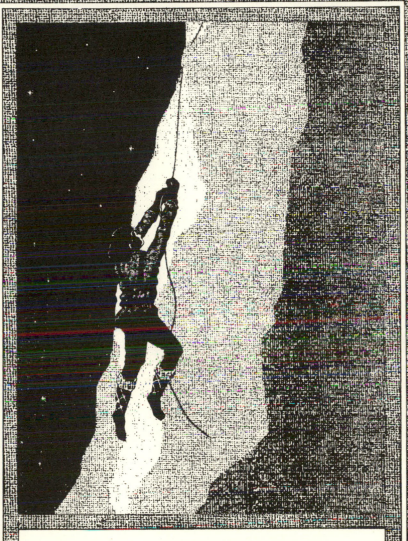

The Prince felt as though he were dying. He had been to the top of Arras, but he suddenly doubted he would ever live to see the lower slopes.

The excitement of the King's camp was too intense for any of the men to sleep. By midnight they were watching the Prince move slowly down the ice wall. Steadily throughout the night the green fire moved down the darksome mountain. During the early hours of morning, before the breaking of the day, the light paused.

The King knew that this would be the last great test that Kyrris would have to undergo. Agonizing, he watched his son, knowing that his arms must nearly be destroyed by fatigue as he grasped the iron stakes driven in the stone. How well Gerell understood the agony his son endured.

For Khordez, also, it was a test. Grasping the rope in his teeth, the ferret climbed with it a thousand khronns into the fading stars. Once more he gnawed the distant knots until the filament fell free. The light rope floated down the surface of the cliff.

Down, down, and ever down it fell. A slow and steady plunge that seemed to float in slowness that never would allow it to reach the high and desperate stakes where Kyrris hung.

The Prince looked upward, and in the torture of his fatigue he wondered if he'd have the strength when the time came. At last it did. In an act of daring, he let go with one hand. His free arm flailed the air. As he caught the mass of rope, it tore at him with a brutal jolt.

"So near and yet so far!" thought Kyrris. The Prince felt as though he were dying. He had been to the top of Arras, but he suddenly doubted he would ever live to see the lower slopes. He fought the images of death that began to plague his mind. His arms would fail. His body would plunge a thousand khronns—or ten thousand—to be lost in the deep abyss of the Crevasse of Death. His dream was dying, and he would die just like all the others who had tried to reach the Brotherstone.

The King watched anxiously, as though he could see the pain in the boy's anguished face. But his son still held the rope. And as long as he could do so, both father and son could hope. Feebly and in slow motion, the Prince formed a loop and passed the second knot around his body. Deftly, slowly, with but a single hand, he wound the loop and drew it beneath his shoulders until it was secure.

"My son," called Gerell. "I love you!"

The King observed his son—was it possible that he had heard? The Prince had stopped. Suddenly, Gerell knew that he must try again.

"Son . . ." his volume grew as he shouted straight upward. "Son . . . I love you!"

The King waited. He watched his son stare downward, past the dark stone slopes. Prince Kyrris strained to behold the ground that flanked the cliffs.

"Father?" the voice seemed to emanate from the very center of the green fire.

"Father . . . Father!"

The voice called again louder and more clearly. The silent night moved back. There was no sound at all except for the clear strong voice of an anguished youth who hung upon an iron spike an eternity above.

"Father . . . Do you live in the darkness? I cannot see. . . . It is too dark . . ."

"I live in the darkness." Something long forgotten seemed to come alive.

"Father . . ."

The King could barely hear, "Father, do you look this way?"

The father seemed to hear his child and son call in the darkness of so long ago.

He shouted back, "I look your way, my son." The words shot up the stone wall and exploded all around the Prince. Once again, as in his childhood, the glorious words set Kyrris free. He knew that in the darkness, where his eyes had failed to see, his father waited. He knew he must not quit, for his pain was observed and when pain is shared it is bearable.

Kyrris again faced the wall. He felt the rope around his waist and smiled at the comedy of his plan. If he were to fall a thousand khronns, the rope would not be his salvation but his executioner. For even if it didn't break it would slice like a knife into his body, and there his life would end.

Below him, a thousand khronns of rope hung in a doubled arc. Two strands, each half the length of his descent, hung limply side by side. As he worked his way downward, the loop would gradually become a single line that shot straight up the stone precipice to the spike upon which he now hung.

Each one of his boots felt like it weighed a thousand pounds. He decided that the Brotherstone would warm his legs and feet as well as it did his upper torso. Again hanging by only one hand, he unbuckled his boot straps. He removed each boot and dropped it into the blackened void.

His legs felt lighter, but he knew his feet would grow cold as he descended the icy cliffs. He knew he must work fast to reach the Ledge of Legarro before he experienced frostbite.

But could he work fast? He seemed to hear the words all over again, "I look your way, my son."

As soon as Khordez was back he would begin again. Suddenly, the Prince felt guilty . . . he had been so concerned for his own life, he had not given much thought to the ferret. On the icy cliff above, with his paws bleeding from digging through solid ice, Khordez made his way slowly down the cliff.

Kyrris waited. It was not long before he could see the ferret in the green light. Kyrris sensed Khordez was in danger. The ferret moved slowly, his whole body quivering. The Prince feared that his faithful friend would not survive. He agonized for Khordez, without whose help Mt. Arras would have gone unconquered.

The ferret stopped. He shivered as though he could go no further. Kyrris saw that he was locked in his resolve to die there on the mountain—he would not add even his own small weight to the burden that the Prince had to bear.

"All right, little friend—none of this . . . let's go! Come down slowly . . . I can wait."

But Kyrris knew he could not wait for long. His feet would freeze against the icy cliff. When the ferret refused to move, Kyrris gave a firm command. "Come Khordez, this instant!"

The ferret tried to obey; he moved down the vertical stone . . . his feet, small as they were, could no longer grasp even a little of the ice. His muscles, like those of his master, were refusing to obey. His paws were numbed, and he slipped a frightful distance before he could grab hold again.

Kyrris looked on intently. He swung outward from the spike on which he clung while his eyes remained riveted to the ferret.

Khordez slipped again. He could not hold. He shrieked a piteous scream, as though begging the Prince's help. His cry in the green light seemed to pierce the heart of Kyrris. The eyes of the ferret pleaded with those of his master. It was a silent and a final plea. A brown-red ball of fur hurtled toward the light below.

In pain, Kyrris stretched his hand outward. The ferret

struck his hand and rebounded into his chest. His tiny claws thrust like hooks there, into the tunic of Kyrris.

He held! But the impact nearly tore Kyrris from the iron stake.

"Into my tunic!" cried Kyrris.

It was a command that Khordez did not need. He quickly swung inside the tunic of the Prince and peered out over the collar. Kyrris coiled the rope on his waist and leaned outward. Gradually, he forced his numb, almost paralyzed left hand to release the iron stake. He flexed his arm and rotated it to relieve the pain. At last he started down.

When the green light began to move down the mountain again, a volley of cheers broke through the stillness of the night. There was dancing and laughter in the camp of Gerell. The Gallactors were so excited that their cheers rose high into the green light. Kyrris heard, and dropped even more rapidly and with confidence toward the ground below.

Just before daybreak the Prince felt the marvelous thrill of his bare feet on the ledge of stone. Even as his naked feet touched the Ledge of Legarro, a second volley of cheers exploded into the sky.

Kyrris collapsed on the ledge and placed the green fire against his nearly frozen feet. The ledge grew warm. For a few hours the son of Gerell slept. . . .

"You have a deadly fever, son," he heard his father say.

"Father, I feel fine."

"Your sickness is the Brotherstone," said Gerell, but not loudly enough to wake the sleeping Kyrris.

As he slept he was bathed in two very beautiful lights—one as green and pure as the light could be, and the other as gold and warm as the bright sun of Krissandor could make it.

From the city of Krissandor the loyal subjects of Gerell had watched the green light move down the mountain. They had never known a time that the green glow of the Brotherstone had not illuminated the icy peak. Now the top of Arras was dark and the light was at last coming to live among the people.

The excitement was all the King could bear. At daybreak, streams of people began to leave the city, moving across the plains toward the mountain.

The Prince slept on, unaware of their coming. About noon he awoke, feeling warm and new. He looked upward and saw the small cord. It seemed a million khronns. He was inclined at first to doubt that he had made the trip at all, until he looked at his hands—they were cut nearly to shreds by all that they had endured.

He was not far from the Crevasse of Death. Beyond it lay the camp of Gerell. He could see that they were all watching him. No sooner had he stood than all of them began to cheer once more.

Kyrris smiled at their rejoicing. Once more he strapped the Brotherstone to his back. Khordez sat on his shoulder, and the Prince began to make his way downward. In two brief hours, he crossed the vertical but heavily ridged wall between the Ledge of Legarro and the Crevasse of Death. At long last, he faced his father across the chasm.

The jubilant King had tears of joy on his face. His triumphant son smiled.

"Father, my rope is up there. How do I get across?" asked Kyrris.

"Pellen will see to that!" replied his father.

Pellen drew an arrow and attached a cord to it. To the cord he tied a rope. Pellen shot the arrow into the air and it flew across the crevasse landing harmlessly near Kyrris's feet. Kyrris picked up the arrow and cord, and pulled the rope across the dark and bottomless void. When the rope was secure, Kyrris grabbed it and swung joyfully over the chasm, climbing upward to gain the ledge. He was safe!

The enthusiastic Gallactors grabbed his arms and lifted him to the camp. His father ran to him, and the two embraced in joy.

"Father, Arras is conquered. The Brotherstone is yours!"

As they journeyed back to the city, the people of the kingdom erupted in the joy of the new green light. There was dancing in every street and lane.

"Kyrris lives! He brings the Brotherstone to Krissandor!"

VII

The Voyage

The length of the sky may be light years away
And yet bonded by unseen emotions above;
The distance will trade the light years for days
And worlds are brought nearer by love.

"It is a sign between us."

The winter snows came early. As the Festival drew near, the land was white from the seas to the mountains. The Brotherstone was set upon a pedestal of marble before the palace.

The King announced that every man, woman, and child throughout the entire realm should gather in the courtyard for the Winter Festival. When the star appeared, the realm of Krissandor would stand as one to send the Brotherstone to teach the darker skies of love.

Then Gerell called Prince Kyrris and asked him once again if he could bear the voyage and the lonely vigil he would keep, one thousand stars from home.

"As long as it is not forever," said the Prince.

"It is only for a while," the King promised. "Where you are bound, the years are so short that your sojourn will seem but one of our days."

"You want this so much, do you not, Father?" asked the Prince.

"Until that unhappy world learns of love and peace, I cannot be fulfilled," said Gerell.

"When will I go?" asked the son.

"When the evening star is born above Mt. Arras," replied the father.

"Before I go, I have a favor to ask of you."

"What is it, son!"

71

Prince Kyrris reached into his tunic. Khordez came out reluctantly. The Prince handed him to the King.

"Here is the hero of Mt. Arras. Care for him till I return. . . . The people are gathering outside the castle, Father. Shall we go out?"

"Before we do, I want to show you this."

His father reached inside his own tunic and drew out a white bird.

"Mother's white dove . . . what does this mean, Father?" asked Kyrris.

"It is a sign between us. When next you see this bird you will be in the other world. This bird will be for you a sign of great assurance. It will be the reminder that you are my son—and nothing that happens in any world can change this."

Kyrris held the dove and the two men walked outside. Thousands of Gerell's subjects waited in the snow, watching as the King and Prince walked to the Brotherstone.

Gerell raised his hand and brought it down upon the Brotherstone as though his arm were a cleaver and his hand the blade. The stone split in two. He extended his left hand, which held the dove, and said to all assembled, "Here is the seal between two worlds. He shall accompany my son on the journey past a thousand stars."

The beautiful bird, as white as the palace grounds, fluttered into the night sky and soon was lost among the stars.

"Kyrris, my son," said Gerell, turning to the Prince. The boy walked to his father.

Gerell touched him, and though he felt no pain, Kyrris dwindled in size before the multitude. When finally he was smaller than the dove, his father stopped and picked him up and placed him on his right hand.

"There's a needy world out there," said Gerell, pointing into the night sky.

He placed his son between the separated halves of the Brotherstone. He then reached down and closed the halves, restoring in green fire the broken hemisphere.

The thousands who gathered for the Festival of the evening star stood silent before the drama they had witnessed. The Prince was gone, absorbed within the stone that blazed with such a bright incandescence that few could behold it.

The King could see that the distant evening star was rising over Mt. Arras. Since the mountain was now void of the emerald light, the star was easier to see.

"Let the Festival of Stars begin!" cried Gerell.

With one voice, the host of Krissandor began to sing. And even as they did the brilliant, gleaming Brotherstone began to rise . . . slowly at first.

Here is the Festival of Stars!
Now reigns our once and glorious King!
Come and behold Him
Whose splendor is light—
Whose scepter is joyous day—
Whose coming dispels the gathering night,
Whose chariots fly where the bright planets play!

Come, children, come all!
Now gather! Now sing!
For this is the Day of the King!

The Brotherstone now hung in space, as though reluctant for its voyage. Silhouetted against the night, it seemed a bright gem whose green fire fell in shimmering rays of splendor.

"Go!" cried King Gerell. "And may the ancient stars guard you, my son. Though the voyage will be long, when all this enterprise is done, none ever will doubt that Gerell is the King of Love . . ." He stopped for a moment and turned to the multitude, saying, "This is my Son whom I love and in whom I take pleasure." Then he spoke to the Brotherstone as if to speak inside the stone.

"Go now, for this is the Day of the King!"

The emerald light rose higher and higher until it was but a star set bold against the night. In a stream of brilliant fire it flashed across the peak of Arras and was gone.

Gerell walked slowly back into the castle as the crowd began to disperse. As his feet fell upon the new snow, he knew he would see Prince Kyrris again, and the Brotherstone—so long the light of Arras—was free to shed its brilliance in another world! His mood was as quiet as the stars, yet bright as the snow of winter.

Suddenly, Khordez scampered out of the castle and

ran to Gerell. The old King reached to pick him up, but the ferret evaded his grasp and dashed back into the palace. The King sensed that he wished for him to follow, and so he did. Gerell traced the lower corridors of the palace and soon discovered Khordez was heading for the castle gallery, where a new green star had just appeared.

When the King arrived in the great dark hall of space he sat down, and Khordez climbed upon his shoulder. There it was: a small pinpoint of light moving through the fields of stars!

Khordez made a ferret's cry of joy and then fell silent . . . between two vast and separate worlds there flew the Brotherstone . . .

"It is the Day of the King," said Gerell.

The gallery was hushed by the flight of the swift green star.

EPILOGUE

The Day of the King

Wherever Wise Men pray and wait
And love the stars . . . adore the night . . .
The skies at last will yield to faith
And dark will celebrate the light.

"I cannot say that stars direct destinies or mark kings.
Truth, like either one, must have its source and purest
origin beyond our present world."

Blackness closed in.

The fire was gone and only the ashes marked where it had been. The old ones sat as still as the dark hulks of their tents. Balthazar's voice had died gradually during the telling of his tale, until his final words were whispered syllables separated by long silences.

"Look!" Slowly and with deliberation, Kaspar raised his arm and pointed toward the dead, dark city in the distance. In the heavens they saw the rebirth of the same star that they had been following for months.

In wonder they watched the lost, fierce light wink on in the sky. They raised their old faces and studied it as it grew in its brightness.

"Notice, Balthazar," protested Melchior, "it is not green! If anything, it holds a fine blue fire."

"Who would ever believe such a story?" said Kaspar.

Balthazar struggled free of his reverie. Joining the nearer world of his two companions, he gestured toward the sky and said, "It is easy for me to believe that all of this is but the gallery of some great universal lover. It is not the stars which order the courses of men," protested Balthazar, "but a great, loving King who orders the courses of both."

They all were silent now, mulling the wisdom of the ancient sage.

"I think the star is moving," said Melchior at last, turning his eyes full into the upper light.

"Balthazar, is the story you have told true?" It was not a profound question for a wise man to ask.

"True?" puzzled Balthazar.

"True . . ." he repeated. "What does 'true' mean? Does it mean that the enchanter who first told it to our villages believed his tale? If so, the story is true."

"You are stalling . . . true or not?"

"How can we ever measure if there are other stars or suns?" came the reply. "How can we ever prove there is a universal King who gives his Son so freely to souls that Son has never seen? This much is true: A King has been born and you may be sure he himself will be the truth." There was another pause. The great star blazed bold in the heavens.

"Well," said Balthazar at last, "I cannot say that stars direct destinies or mark kings. Truth, like either one, must have its source and purest origin beyond our present world. There is nothing truer than this tale, I assure you."

"Look, the star is moving!" cried Melchior. "It crosses the city and moves on toward the southeast."

"It moves toward Bethlehem," said Balthazar. "While we have the light, let us rouse the caravans and follow."

"Even if it is blue and not green?" smiled Kaspar.

"Perhaps in this Bethlehem we shall test the tale," replied Balthazar. "Perhaps there, where the light shines, we will find the truth."

"Indeed, where the light shines is always the best place

to look for truth." He put the big emerald in his pouch. He felt confident the blue-white star that now moved silently across the dark city toward the little town was witness to a greater truth than any of them could imagine.

"My friend, what if in that little town we should meet the Son of a great King?" asked Kaspar.

Balthazar did not answer. He felt the stone inside his pouch and thought of the land he had spoken of in his story. Old men rarely sing out loud, but an inner melody warmed his heart as he shuffled silently toward the caravan. This inner music spilled through every fissure of his bent frame: it came not from the stars, but their Maker. "Wise men know the best songs," thought Balthazar. "The heart can keep a melody even when the stars doubt it . . . yes . . .

> Here is the Festival of Stars!
> Now reigns our once and glorious King!
> Come and behold Him
> Whose splendor is light—
> Whose scepter is joyous day—
> Whose coming dispels the gathering night—
> Whose chariots fly where the bright planets play!
> Come children, come all!
> Now gather! Now sing!
> For this is the Day of the King!

11-8-85 Jim Derlt